PRECIOUS PROMISES

Joseph Alleine

THE BANNER OF TRUTH TRUST

THE BANNER OF TRUTH TRUST

Head Office
3 Murrayfield Road
Edinburgh, EH12 6EL
UK

North America Office
PO Box 621
Carlisle, PA 17013
USA

banneroftruth.org

Originally published as two chapters in
Heaven Opened; or, A Brief and Plain Discovery of the Riches of God's Covenant of Grace, by Richard Alleine (1665).

This version is based on the edition published by
The Religious Tract Society (London, 1836). The text has been lightly edited, archaic forms have been updated and explanatory footnotes have been added.

*

ISBN
Print: 978 1 80040 019 1
EPUB: 978 1 80040 020 7
Kindle: 978 1 80040 021 4

*

Typeset in 10.5 / 13.5 Adobe Garamond Pro
at The Banner of Truth Trust, Edinburgh

Printed in the UK by
Buchanan McPherson Ltd.,
Hamilton

FOREWORD

This little booklet is a devotional classic. It is well known that Augustine's *Confessions* is one long prayer, in which the author pours out his heart to his Creator in confession, question and praise. Joseph Alleine, a young Puritan minister of the seventeenth century, wrote another most remarkable first-person narrative, but with some crucial differences to Augustine's. It is much shorter than *The Confessions*. It doesn't recount a human autobiography. It is not presented as the author's words to God, but rather as God's words to all Christian believers. In these pages Alleine quotes or paraphrases many of God's promises to his people, and organizes them into a clear and helpful gospel 'map.'

First printed after his death by his father-in-law, Richard Alleine, as two chapters in his own work *Heaven Opened* (1665), they have often been appreciated on their own as a separate little publication. In the pages that follow you will discover how the author gathers divine assurance for the great comfort of believers. Alleine's pastorally sensitive handling of God's precious promises has proved to be a favourite balm and encouragement to weary and tired souls in our own congregation. May you find it to be so, too.

MARK DEVER
Pastor, Capitol Hill Baptist Church
Washington DC
January 2021

PRECIOUS PROMISES

PART ONE

THE RICHES OF THE COVENANT,

OR,

**A SHORT VIEW OF THE EXCEEDING GREAT AND
PRECIOUS PROMISES.**

*God speaking from Mount Gerazim; or the gospel in a map: being
a short view of the exceeding great and precious promises by another
hand.*

The Voice of the Herald

O all inhabitants of the world and dwellers on the earth: come
see and hear. Gather yourselves together for the proclamation of
the great king. Hear, you who are far off and you who are near. He
who has an ear to hear, let him hear. I am the voice of one crying
in the wilderness, Prepare the way of the Lord. Let every valley be
exalted, and every mountain made low, for the glory of the Lord
is to be revealed. Go through, go through the gates, prepare the
way. Cast up, cast up the highway; gather out the stones, lift up
the standard for the people; for the Lord proclaims salvation to the
ends of the earth. Good news, good news, O captives! Hear, all you
who look for salvation in Israel; behold, I bring you glad tidings
of great joy, which shall be for all people. Blessed news! prepare

your ears and hearts. The Lord has commanded me, saying, Go to the people and sanctify them; let them wash and be ready, for the Lord is coming down upon Mount Zion, in the sight of all the nations. Not in earthquakes and fire, not in clouds and darkness, not in thunderings and burnings, tearing apart the mountains and breaking the rocks in pieces. He does not speak to you out of the blackness and darkness and tempest; you shall say no more, Let not God speak to us, lest we die. He comes peaceably, the law of kindness is in his mouth, he preaches Peace, peace, to him who is far off, and to him who is near.

Behold how he comes, leaping upon the mountains. He has passed Mount Ebal—no more wrath or cursing; he has come to Mount Gerizim, where he stands to bless the people. As Mordecai did to his nation, he writes the words of truth and peace, seeking the welfare of his people and speaking peace to all his seed.

Behold how he comes, clothed with flames of love, with a heart of compassion, plenteous redemption, and multiplied pardons. O how full is his love! O the tenderness of his compassions! O how full is his heart, even aching till it is eased by supplying his hungry children!

Listen carefully therefore, O children, listen to me. To you it is commanded, O people, nations, and languages, that whenever you hear the joyful sound, the trumpet of jubilee, the good news of peace in the voice of the everlasting gospel, that you fall down before the throne, and worship him who lives for ever and ever.

Arise, and come away. Prepare, prepare yourselves. Do not hear with an uncircumcised ear; you are not dealing with a common thing. Behold, the throne is set, the throne of grace, where majesty and mercy dwell together; from there the Lord will meet you, from there he will commune with you, from the mercy seat, from between the cherubim, upon the ark of the testimony. Lo, the Lord comes out of his pavilion, the mighty God from Zion.

Selah. His glory covers the heavens, the earth is full of his praise. A fire of love goes before him, mercy and truth are round about him, righteousness and peace are the habitation of his throne; he rides on his horses and chariots of salvation, the covenant of life and peace is in his mouth.

Rejoice, you heavens, make a joyful noise to the Lord, all the earth. Let the sea roar, the floods clap their hands, and the multitude of the isles rejoice. Stand forth, the host of heaven, prepare your harps, cast down your crowns, be ready with your trumpets, bring forth your golden bowls full of sweet smelling aromas; for our voices will jar, our strings will break, we cannot reach the note of our Maker's praise.

Yet let them who dwell in the dust arise and sing. Bear your part in this glorious service, but consider and pay attention. Call out your souls, and all that is within you. Lift up your voices, fix your eyes, enlarge your hearts, exert all their powers; there is work for them all. Be intent and serious, you cannot strain too high.

Come forth, you graces, pave the way, be all in readiness. Stand forth, faith and hope: flame O love, come you warm desires, and break with longing. Let fear with all veneration pay its respectful obedience. Joy prepare your songs, call up all the daughters of music to salute the Lord as he passes by. Let the generations of the saints appear, and spread the way with boughs and garments of salvation, and songs of deliverance. You stand this day all of you before the Lord your God, your captains, your elders, your officers, with all the men of Israel, your little ones, your wives, and the stranger who is within your camp, from the hewer of wood to the drawer of water. That you should enter into covenant with the Lord your God, and into his oath which the Lord your God makes with you this day: that he may establish you today as a people for himself, and that he may be your God, as he has said to you, and as he has sworn (Deut. 29:10-13).

I have done my errand. The messenger of the morning disappears; when the rising sun comes forth out of his chambers, I vanish. I put my mouth in the dust. The voice of the Lord! The soft and still voice! O my soul, wrap your face in your outer garment, and bow yourself to the ground, and put yourself in the cleft of the rock, while Jehovah proclaims his name, and makes all his goodness to pass before you.

The Voice of the Lord

Hear, O ends of the earth, the mighty God, the Lord has spoken: Gather my saints to me; those that have made a covenant with me by sacrifice (Psa. 50:1, 5). Behold, I establish my covenant between me and you (Gen. 17:7). By my holiness have I sworn, that I will be your covenant friend. I lift up my hand to heaven, I swear that I live for ever; and because I live, you shall live also (John 14:19). I will be yours (Jer. 32:38-40): yours to all intents and purposes: your refuge and your rest (Jer. 50:6; Psa. 90:1; Psa. 46:1); your patron and your portion (Psa. 73:26; Isa. 25:4, 5); your heritage and your hope; your God and your guide (Psa. 48:14). While I have, you shall never want; and what I am to myself, I will be to you (Psa. 34:9, 10). And you shall be my people, a chosen generation, a kingdom of priests, a holy nation, a peculiar treasure unto me above all people (Exod. 19:5, 6; 1 Pet. 2:9). I call heaven and earth to witness this day, that I take you to be mine forever. My name shall be upon you, and you shall be pillars in the temple of your God, and shall go no more out (Rev. 3:12).

My special uniform shall you wear, and the stamp of my own face shall you carry (Ezek. 36:25, 26, with Eph. 4:24); and I will make you my witnesses, and the epistles of Christ to the world (2 Cor. 3:3), and you shall be chosen vessels to bear my name before the sons of men. And that you may see that I am in earnest with you, lo, I make with you an everlasting covenant, ordered in all things, and sure (2 Sam. 23:5); and do here solemnly deliver it to you as my act and deed, sealed with sacred blood (1 Cor. 11:25), and ratified with the oath of a God (Heb. 6:17); a God who cannot lie, who knows no place for repentance (Titus 1:2). Come, you blessed, receive the instrument of your salvation; take the writings, behold the seals; here are the conveyances of the kingdom. Fear not, the donation is free and full. See, it is written in blood, founded on the all-sufficient merits of your Surety (Heb. 9), in whom I am well pleased (Matt. 3:17); whose death makes this testament unchangeable for ever; so that your names can never be put out, nor your inheritance alienated, nor your legacies diminished; nothing may be altered, nothing added, nothing subtracted, no, not for ever (Gal. 3:15-17).

The blessings of the covenant are either its glorious liberties and immunities or its royal privileges and prerogatives.

Happy are you, O Israel! Who is like you, O people! (Deut. 33:29). Only believe, and know your own blessedness. Give attention, O my children, to the blessings of your Father; and hear and know the *glorious immunities*, and the *royal prerogatives* that I here confirm upon you.

The immunities and liberties of the covenant, consisting in:

1. *Our general discharge from all our debts.*

Here I seal *your pardons*. Though your sins be as many as the sands, and as mighty as the mountains, I will drown them in the depths of my bottomless mercies (Mic. 7:19). I will be merciful to your unrighteousness; I will multiply pardons (Heb. 8:12; Isa. 55:7); where your sins have abounded, my grace shall superabound; though they be as scarlet, they shall be as white as snow; though red like crimson, they shall be as wool (Isa. 1:18). Behold, I declare myself satisfied, and pronounce you absolved (Job 33:24). The price is paid, your debts are cleared, your bonds are cancelled (Isa. 43:25; Col. 2:13, 14).

Whatever the law, or conscience, or the accuser has to charge upon you, here I exonerate you, I discharge you. I, even I, am he who blots out your transgressions, for my name's sake. Who shall lay anything to your charge, when I acquit you? Who shall impeach or plead against you, when I proclaim you guiltless? (Rom. 8:33, 34). Sons, daughters, be of good cheer; your sins are forgiven you (1 John 2:12; Mark 9:2). I will sprinkle your consciences, and put the voice of peace into their mouths (Ezek. 36:25; Heb. 9:14; Isa. 57:19), and they shall be your registers, in which I will record your pardon, and the voice of guilt and wrath and terror shall cease (Heb. 10:22; Isa. 27:4, 5).

2. *Our release from the house of bondage particularly.*

Here I sign *your release from the house of bondage* (Rom. 6:17, 18; 1 Cor. 7:22). Come forth you captives, come forth you prisoners of hope, for I have found a ransom (Job 33:24, 18), I proclaim liberty to the captives, and the opening of the prison to those who are bound (Isa. 61:1; 42:7). Behold, I have broken your chains, and shaken the foundations of your prisons, and opened the iron gates (Luke 4:18). By the blood of the covenant I have sent forth the prisoners out of the pit in which there was no water (Zech. 9:11). Arise, O redeemed of the Lord, put off the clothes of your captivities, arise and come away.

From the dark and noisome prison of sin.

The dark and noisome *prison of sin* shall no longer detain you (John 8:34-36). I will loose your fetters, and knock off your bolts. Sin shall not have dominion over you (Rom. 6:14).

I will heal your backslidings, I will subdue your iniquities (Mic. 7:19; Jer. 3:12), I will sanctify you wholly (1 Thess. 5:23, 24), and will put my fear in your hearts, that you shall not depart from me (Jer. 32:40). Though your corruptions be strong and many, yet the aids of my Spirit, and cleansing virtue of my word, and strong medicine of my corrections, shall so work together with your prayers and endeavours, that they shall not finally prevail against you, but shall surely fall before you (Ezek. 36:37; Eph. 5:26; Isa. 27:9).

From the strong and stinking jail of the grave.

From the strong and stinking *jail of the grave* I deliver you. O death, I will be your plague; O grave, I will be your destruction (Hos. 13:14); my beloved shall never see corruption (Psa. 16:10). I will change your rottenness into glory, and make your dust arise and praise me (Dan. 12:2, 3; Isa. 26:19). What is sown in weakness, I will raise in power; what is sown in corruption, I will raise in incorruption; what is sown a natural body, I will raise a spiritual body (1 Cor. 15:42-44). This very flesh of yours, this corruptible flesh, shall put on incorruption, and this mortal shall put on immortality (1 Cor. 15:53). Death shall be swallowed up in victory, and mortality of life (1 Cor. 15:54; 2 Cor. 5:4). Fear not, O my children. Come, and I will show you the enemy that you dreaded. See, here lies the king of terrors, like Sisera in the tent, fastened to the ground with the nail struck through his temples. Behold the grateful present, the head of your enemy on a platter: I bequeath you your conquered adversary, and make over death as your legacy (1 Cor. 3:22). O death, where is your sting? where now is your armour in which you trusted? (1 Cor. 15:55). Come, my people, enter into your chambers (Isa. 26:20). Come to your beds of dust, and lie down in peace, and let your flesh rest in hope (Isa. 57:2); for even in this flesh shall you see God (Psa. 16:9; Job 19:25-27). O you slain of death, your carcasses, now as loathsome as the carrion in the ditch, will I redeem from the power of the grave (Psa. 49:15), and transform those vile bodies to be like the glorious body of your exalted Redeemer (Phil. 3:21). Look, if you can, on the sun when shining in his strength; with such dazzling glory will I clothe you, O you of little faith (Matt. 13:43).

From the dungeon of eternal darkness.

From the *terrible dungeon of eternal darkness* I hereby free you. Fear not, you shall not be hurt by the second death (Rev. 2:11; Rom. 8:1); you are delivered from the wrath to come, and shall never come into condemnation (1 Thess. 1:10; John 5:24). The flames of Tophet[1] shall not be able to singe the hairs of your heads, no, nor the smell of fire pass upon you. Stand upon the brink, and look down into the horrible pit, the infernal prison, from which I have freed you. Do you see how the smoke of their torments ascends for ever? (Rev. 14:11). Do you hear the cursings and ravings, the roarings and blasphemies? (Matt. 25:30). What do you think of those hellish fiends? Would you have been willing to have them for your companions and tormentors? (Matt. 25:41). What do you think of those chains of darkness, of the river of brimstone, of the instruments of torment for soul and body, of those weepings and wailings and gnashing of teeth? Can you think of an everlasting banishment, of a 'Go you cursed?' Could you dwell with everlasting burnings, could you abide with devouring fire? (Isa. 33:14). This is the inheritance you were born to (Eph. 2:3). But I have cut off the entail, and wrought for you a great salvation. I have not ordained you to wrath (1 Thess. 5:9), but my thoughts towards you are thoughts of peace (Jer. 29:11).

3. *Our protection from all our enemies.*

Here I deliver you *your protection*. From all your enemies will I save you (2 Kings 17:39).

---

[1] Tophet = a place of burning and a synonym for Hell.

From the arrests of the law.

I grant you a protection from the arrests of the law: your Surety has fully answered it (Gal. 3:13; Rom. 5:10); my justice is satisfied, my wrath is pacified, my honour is repaired (Dan. 2:24; 2 Cor. 5:19, 20). Behold, I am near who justifies you; who is he that shall condemn you?

From the powers of darkness.

From the *usurped dominion of the powers of darkness*. I will tread Satan shortly under you, and will set your feet in triumph upon the necks of your enemies (Rom. 16:20). Let not your hearts be troubled, though you must wrestle with principalities and powers, and the rulers of the darkness of this world (Eph. 6:12); for stronger is he that is in you, than he that is in the world (1 John 4:4). He may bruise your heel, but you shall bruise his head (Gen. 3:15). Behold your Redeemer leading captivity captive, spoiling principalities and powers, and triumphing over them openly in his cross (Col. 2:15). See how Satan falls like lightning from heaven (Luke 10:18), and the Samson of your salvation bears away the gates of hell, posts and all, upon his shoulders, and sets them up as trophies of his victory: how he pulls out the throat of the lion, and lifts up the heart of the traitor upon the top of his spear, and washes his hands, and dyes his robes in the blood of those who are your enemies (Isa. 63:1-3).

From the victory of the world.

From the *victory of the world* (1 John 5:4; Gal. 1:4). Neither its frowns nor its flatteries shall be too hard for your victorious faith. Though it raise up Egypt and Amalek and Moab, and all its armies against you: yet it shall never keep you out of Canaan. Be of good comfort, your Lord has overcome the world (John 16:33). Though its temptations be very powerful, yet this, upon my faithfulness, will I promise you, that nothing shall come upon you but what you shall be able to bear. But if I see such trials, which you fear would be too hard for your graces, and would overthrow your souls, I will never allow them to come upon you; no, I will make your enemy to serve you (1 Cor. 10:13), and I will bequeath the world as part of your dowry to you (1 Cor. 3:22).

From the curse of the cross.

From the *curse of the cross* (Psa. 119:71). Affliction shall prove a wholesome cup to you; your Lord has drunk the venom into his own body, and what remains for you is but a healthy potion, which I will promise you shall work for your good (Rom. 8:28). Do not be afraid to drink, and do not desire that the cup should pass from you: I bless the cup before I give it unto you (Job 5:17, etc.). Drink all of it, and be thankful; you shall find my blessing at the bottom of the cup, to sweeten the sharpest afflictions for you (James 1:12; Psa. 94:12). I will stand by you in all conditions, and be a firm friend to you in every change (Isa. 43:2). In the wilderness I will speak comfortably to you, and in the fire and in the water I will be with you (Hos. 2:14). I will be a strength to the poor, and a strength to the needy in his distress; a refuge from the storm, and a shadow from the heat, when the blast of those who terrify you is as a storm against the wall (Isa. 25:4). Your sufferings shall not be a cup of wrath, but a grace cup; not a curse, but a cure; not a cup of trembling, but a cup of blessing to you (Heb. 12:6-8). They shall not hurt you, but heal you (Psa. 119:67). My blessing shall attend you in every condition (Gen. 26:3). I say not only, blessed shall you be in your basket, and blessed in your store; but blessed shall you be in your poverty (Gen. 28:15), and blessed shall you be in your straits: not only blessed shall you be in your cities, and blessed shall you be in your fields; but blessed shall you be in your bonds, and blessed shall you be in your banishment (Mark 10:29, 30; 1 Pet. 3:14). Blessed shall you be when you are persecuted, and when you are reviled, and your name is cast out as evil; yes, then doubly blessed (Matt. 5:10-12). My choicest blessings, greatest good, and richest sweets, will I put into your evil things (1 Pet. 4:13, 14; Luke 6:20-22). These happy immunities, these glorious liberties of the sons of God, by this immutable charter I do for ever settle upon you; and do in and with my covenant unalterably, irrevocably, everlastingly convey to you, and confirm upon you.

The privileges and prerogatives of the covenant.

Yea, I will not only free you from your miseries, but will confer upon you *royal privileges and prerogatives*, and install you into higher and greater happiness than you have ever fallen from. Lo, I give *myself* to you, and *all things* with myself.

1. *He gives himself to us to be our God.*

Behold, O sons of men! Behold, and wonder! Be astonished, O heavens! Be moved, you strong foundations of the earth! For you shall be my witnesses. This day by covenant I give *myself* to my servants (Gen. 17:7). I will be your God for ever and ever (Psa. 48:14; Jer. 32:38; Rev. 21:3). Your own God (Psa. 67:6; 16:2). Nothing in the world is so much your own as I. The houses that you have built, that you have bought, are not so much yours as I am. Here you are tenants at will; but I am your eternal inheritance (Psa. 16:5 with 73:26). These are loans for a season, but I am your dwelling-place in all generations (Psa. 90:1).

To be to us instead of all relations.

You have nowhere so great a propriety, so sure and unalterable a claim, as you have here. What do you count your own? Do you count your bodies your own, your souls your own? No, these are not your own; they are bought with a price (1 Cor. 6:19, 20). But you may boldly make your claim to me; you may freely lay claim to an interest in me (Jer. 3:19; Isa. 63:16). Come near, and fear not; where should you be free, if not with your own? Where should you be bold, if not at home? You are never in all the world so much at home as when you are with me. You may freely make use of me, or of any of my attributes, whenever you need (Psa. 50:15; Jer. 49:11; Psa. 145:18). I will be all to you that you can wish.

Our Friend.

I will be a *Friend* to you (Isa. 41:8; James 2:2, 3). My secrets shall be with you (Psa. 25:14; John 15:15), and you shall have all freedom of access to me, and liberty to pour out all your hearts into my bosom (Eph. 3:12; Heb 4:16).

Our Physician.

I will be a *Physician* to you. I will heal your backslidings, and cure all your diseases (Hos. 14:4; Psa. 103:3). Fear not; never did a soul miscarry that left itself in my hands, and would but follow my prescriptions.

Our Shepherd.

I will be a *Shepherd* to you (Psa. 23:1; 80:1). Do not be afraid of bad news, for I am with you; my rod and my staff shall comfort you. You shall not want, for I will feed you; you shall not wander, to be lost, for I will restore you. I will cause you to lie down in green pastures, and lead you beside the still waters (Psa. 23). I will gather you with my arm, and carry you in my bosom, and will lead on softly, as the flock and the children are able to endure (Isa. 40:11; Gen. 33:13, 14). If officers be careless, I will do the work myself. I will judge between cattle and cattle. I will seek that which was lost, and bring again that which was driven away, and bind up that which was broken, and strengthen that which was sick; but I will destroy the fat and the strong, and will feed them with judgment (Ezek. 34:16, 17 with verses 2-4). I will watch over my flock by night (Isa. 27:3). Behold, I have appointed my ministers as your watchmen, and overseers that watch for your souls (Heb. 13:17; Acts 20:28). Yes, my angels shall be your watchers, and shall keep a constant guard upon my flock (Dan. 3:17, 23; Psa. 34:7). And if perhaps the servants should sleep (Matt. 13:25, 27), my own eyes shall keep a perpetual watch over you, by night and by day (Psa. 34:15; 33:18; 2 Chron. 16:9). The keeper of Israel never slumbers, nor sleeps (Psa. 121:3-5), nor withdraws his eyes from the righteous (Job 36:7). I will guide you with my eye; I will never trust you out of my own sight (Psa. 32:8).

Our Sovereign.

I will be a *Sovereign* to you. The Lord is your judge, the Lord is your lawgiver, the Lord is your king (Isa. 33:22). Fear not the unrighteousness of men, I will judge your cause, I will defend your rights (Deut. 32:36; Psa. 140:12; 9:4). You shall not stand at man's bar; you shall not be cast at their vote (1 Cor. 4:3, 5; 2 Cor. 10:18): let them curse, I will bless; let them condemn, I will justify (Isa. 50:9; Gen. 12:3).

When you come to trial for your lives, to have your eternal state decided, you shall see your *Friend*, your *Father*, upon the bench (Psa. 80:9; Eccles. 3:16, 17). Into my hands shall your cause be cast, and you shall surely stand in judgment, and be found at the right hand among the sheep, and hear the King say, Come you blessed, inherit the kingdom (Matt. 25:33, 34).

Our Husband.

I will be a *Husband* to you (Isa. 54:5). In loving-kindness, and in mercies, will I betroth you to me for ever (Hos. 2:19, 20). I will espouse your interest, and will be as one with you, and you with me (Matt. 25:40, 45; Acts 9:4, 5). You shall be for me, and not for another; and I also will be for you (Hos. 3:3). Though I found you as a helpless infant exposed in its blood, all your unworthiness does not discourage me. Lo, I have looked on you, and put my beauty upon you. Moreover, I swear to you, and enter into covenant with you, and you shall be mine (Ezek. 16:4-10). Behold, I do, as it were, put myself out of my own power, and do here solemnly, in this my marriage covenant, give away myself to you (Jer. 24:7; 30:21, 22; 31:33, 34), and with myself all things (Rev. 21:7). I will be an everlasting portion to you (Ezek. 44:28; Jer. 51:19; Psa. 119:57). Lift up now your eyes eastward, and westward, and northward, and southward. Have you not a worthy portion, a good inheritance? Can you cast up your riches, or count your own happiness? Can you fathom immensity, or reach omnipotency, or comprehend eternity? All this is yours. I will set open all my treasures to you, I will keep back nothing from you.

He makes over himself to us in all his essential perfections and personal relations.

All the attributes in the Godhead, and all the persons in the Godhead, do I hereby make over to you. I will be yours in all my *essential perfections* and in all my *personal relations*.

(1) *In all his essential perfections.*

His eternity as the date of our happiness.

My *eternity* shall be the date of your happiness. I am the eternal God, and while I am, I will be life and blessedness to you (Psa. 90:1, 2 with 48:14; 1 Tim. 1:17 with 1 Pet. 5:10). I will be a never-failing fountain of joy, and peace, and bliss to you (Psa. 36:7-9; 16:11; Isa. 35:10). I am the first and last, that was, and is, and is to come, and my eternal power and Godhead shall be bound to you (Jer. 32:40).

I will be your God, your Father, your Friend, while I have any being (Isa. 9:6; Jer. 10:10). I have made my everlasting choice in selecting you (Psa. 132:13, 14; Hos. 2:19). Fear not, for the eternal God is your refuge, and underneath are the everlasting arms (Deut. 33:27). My durable riches and righteousness shall be yours (Prov. 8:18). Though all should forsake you, yet will I not forsake you (Heb. 13:5; Psa. 27:10). When the world, and all that is in it shall be burned up, I will be a standing portion for you. When you are forgotten among the dead, with everlasting loving-kindness will I remember you (Isa. 54:10).

His unchangeableness as the rock of our rest.

My *unchangeableness* shall be the rock of your rest (Psa. 62:6, 7; 92:15). When all the world is like the tumbling ocean round about you, here you may fix and settle. I am your resting-place (Jer. 50:6; 2 Chron. 14:11).

The *immutability* of my nature, and of my counsel, and of my covenant, are a sure footing for your faith, and a firm foundation for your strong and everlasting consolation (2 Tim. 2:19; Heb. 6:17, 18). When you are afflicted, tossed with tempests (Isa. 54:11), and not comforted; take refuge in to me: I am a haven of hope, I am a harbour of rest for you; here cast your anchors, and you shall never be moved (Jer. 17:13, 17; Psa. 46:1, 2, 5; 125:1).

His omnipotency for our guard.

My *omnipotency* shall be your guard. I am God Almighty, your almighty Protector, your almighty Benefactor (Gen. 15:1; 17:1).

What though your enemies are many, more are they that are with you, than they that are against you; for I am with you (2 Chron. 32:7, 8; 2 Kings 6:16). What though they are mighty, they are not almighty. Your Father is greater than all, and none shall pluck you (pluck as best they can) out of my hands (John 10:29). Who can hinder my power, or obstruct my salvation? (Isa. 43:13;

Dan. 4:35). Who is like the God of Jeshurun, who rides on the heavens for your help, and in his excellency on the sky? I am the shield of your strength, and the sword of your excellency (Deut. 33:26, 29). I am your rock and your fortress, your deliverer, your strength, the horn of your salvation, and your high tower (Psa. 18:2). I will maintain you against all the power of the enemy. You shall never sink, if omnipotency can support you (1 Pet. 1:5). The gates of hell shall not prevail against you (Matt. 16:18). Your enemies shall find hard work of it. They shall overcome victory, or enervate omnipotency, or corrupt fidelity, or change immutability, or else they cannot finally prevail against you; they shall either bow or break (Rev. 3:9; Isa. 66:24). Though they should exalt themselves as the eagle, though they should set their nest among the stars, even from there will I bring them down, says the Lord (Obad. 4; Jer. 49:16).

His faithfulness for our security.

My *faithfulness* shall be your security (Psa. 89:33-35); my truth, yea, my oath shall fail if ever you become a loser because of me (Isa. 54:9, 10 with Mark 10:29, 30). I will make you confess, when you see the outcome and upshot of all my providences, that I was a God worthy to be trusted, worthy to be believed, worthy to be rested in and relied upon (Psa. 34:4-6, 8; 84:12; 146:5; Jer. 17:7, 8; Psa. 22:4, 5). If you do not walk in my judgments, you must look for my threats and frowns, yes, and blows too, and you shall see that I am not in jest with you, nor will indulge you in your sins (Psa. 89:30-32, etc.; Amos 3:2; 2 Sam. 12–15; 1 Pet. 4:17). Nevertheless my loving-kindness I will never take from you, nor allow my faithfulness to fail. My covenant I will not break, nor alter the thing that has gone out from my lips.

His mercies as or store.

My *mercies* shall be your store (Isa. 63:7; Psa. 119:41). I am the Father of mercies, and such a Father I will be to you (2 Cor. 1:3). I am the fountain of mercies, and this fountain shall be ever open to you (Psa. 36:9 with Rev. 21:6).

My mercies are very many, and they shall be multiplied towards you (Neh. 9:17 with Isa. 55:7); very great, and they shall be magnified on you (1 Chron. 21:13 with Gen. 19:19); very sure, and they shall be forever sure to you (Isa. 55:3); very tender, and they shall be infinitely tender towards you (Psa. 119:156 with 103:4). Though the fig tree do not blossom, nor the vine bear, nor the flock bring forth; fear not, for my compassions do not fail (Hab. 3:17; Lam. 3:22). Surely goodness and mercy shall follow you all the days of your lives (Psa. 23:6). Even to your old age I am he, and even to grey hairs will I carry you: I have made, and I will bear, even I will carry and deliver you (Isa. 46:4). I will make an everlasting covenant with you, that I will not turn away from you to do you good (Jer. 32:40). I swear that I will show you the kindness of God (1 Sam. 20:14, 15, 17). I can as soon forget to be God, as forget to be gracious (Psa. 77:9). While my name is Jehovah, merciful, gracious, long-suffering, abundant in goodness and truth, I will never forget to show mercy to you (Psa. 103:17 with 34:6, 7). All my ways towards you shall be mercy and truth (Psa. 25:10). I have sworn that I would not be angry with you, nor rebuke you; for the mountains shall depart, and the hills be removed; but my kindness shall not depart from you, neither shall the covenant of my peace be removed, says the Lord who has mercy on you.

His omnisciency as our overseer.

My *omnisciency* shall be your overseer; my eyes shall be ever open, observing your wants to relieve them, and your wrongs to avenge them (1 Pet. 3:12; Exod. 3:7). My ears shall be ever open to hear the prayers of my poor, the cries of my oppressed, the clamours, calumnies, and reproaches of your enemies (Psa. 34:15; Exod. 2:24, 25; Zeph. 2:8-10). Surely I have seen your affliction, and know your sorrows. And shall not God avenge his own elect? I will avenge them speedily (Luke 18:7, 8). I see the secret plots and designs of your enemies against you (Jer. 18:23), and will disannul their counsels (Isa. 8:10 with 29:14, 15; Psa. 33:10). I see your secret integrity, and the uprightness of your hearts towards me, while the carnal and censorious world condemns you as hypocrites (Job 1:8-11; 2 Chron. 15:17). Your secret prayers, fasts, and tears, which the world does not know, I observe them, and record them (Matt. 6:6, 18; Acts 10:4). Your secret care to please me, your secret pains with your own hearts, your secret self-searchings and self-denial; I see them all, and your Father who sees in secret, shall reward them openly (Matt. 25:34-36; 2 Chron. 34:27).

His wisdom as our counsellor.

My *wisdom* shall be your counsellor. If any lack wisdom, let him ask of me, and it shall be given him (James 1:5). I will be your deliverer. When you are in darkness, I will be a light to you (Mic. 7:8). I will make your way plain before you (Isa. 43:19; 57:14). You are but short-sighted, but I will be eyes to you (Isa. 42:6, 7; 49:6). I will watch over you, to bring upon you all the good I have promised (Jer. 31:28 with 32:24), and to keep off all the evil you fear, or to turn it into good (Psa. 91:10, 14; Jer. 24:5). You shall have your food in its season, and your medicine in its season: mercies, afflictions, all suitable, and in their season (Psa. 23:2, 3; 1 Pet. 1:6; Isa. 27:7-9).

I will outwit your enemies, and make their oracles to speak but folly (Isa. 19:11-15). The old serpent shall not deceive you. I will acquaint you with his devices (2 Cor. 2:11). The deceitful hearts you fear shall not undo you; I will discover their wiles.

I know how to deliver the godly out of temptation, and to reserve the unjust to the day of judgment to be punished (2 Pet. 2:9). Trust in me with all your hearts, and do not lean on your own understanding (Prov. 3:5). I am God who performs all things for you (Psa. 57:2). I will forfeit the reputation of my wisdom, if I make you not to acknowledge, when you see the end of the Lord (James 5:11), (though at present you wonder, and reach not the meaning of my proceedings, Jer. 12:1), that all my works are in weight, and in number, and in time, and in order (Eccles. 3:14): if I cause you not to cry out, Manifold are your works, in wisdom you have made them all (Psa. 33:4; 104:24; 145:10).

His justice as our avenger and rewarder.

My *justice* shall be your revenger and rewarder (2 Thess. 1:6; 2 Tim. 4:8). Fear not to approach; fury is not in me (Isa. 27:4). My justice is not only appeased towards you, but engaged for you. I am so fully satisfied in the sacrifice of my Beloved, that justice itself, which was as a flaming sword drawn against you, now greatly befriends you; and that which was an amazing, confounding terror, shall now become your relief and consolation (Eccles. 3:16, 17; 5:8; Psa. 96:10-14; 97:1 with 99:1). Under all your oppressions, here shall your refuge be (Psa. 6:9; 103:6). Let me know your grievances, my justice shall right your wrongs, and reward your services (Psa. 146:7; Heb. 6:10). You may conclude upon your pardons, conclude upon your crowns, conclude upon reparation for all your injuries, and all from the sweet consideration of my justice (1 John 1:9; 2 Tim. 4:8; 1 Pet. 2:23), the thought of which, to others, is as the horror of the shadow of death. If you sin, do not despair; remember, I am just to forgive you. If you are at any pains or cost for me, do not count it lost; for I am not unrighteous to forget you. I am the righteous Judge, who has laid up for you, and will set on you the crown of righteousness. Are you reviled, persecuted, defamed? Do not forget that I am righteous to render tribulation to those who trouble you, and to you who are troubled, rest with me. Though all your services and sufferings do not deserve the least good at my hands, yet as I have freely passed my promise to reward them, so I will as justly keep it.

His omnipresence as company for us.

My *omnipresence* shall be company for you (1 Chron. 22:18; Josh 1:5, 9; Isa. 41:10). Surely I will be with you, to bless you (Gen. 26:24). No bolts, nor bars, nor bonds, nor banishment, shall remove you from me, nor keep my presence, and the influences of heaven from you (Gen. 39:21, 23). I am always with you (Matt. 28:20): in your darkest nights, in your deepest dangers, I am at hand with you, a very present help in the time of trouble (Psa. 46:1; 34:18). I am not a God afar off, or asleep, or on a journey, when you need my counsel, my ear, or my aid: I am always near to those who fear me.

No Patmos, no prison shall hinder the presence of my grace from you (Rev. 1:9, 10; Acts 16:25, 26). My presence shall perfume the foulest wards, and lighten the darkest dungeon into which you can be thrown (Acts 12:7; Isa. 58:10).

His holiness as a fountain of grace to us.

My *holiness* shall be a fountain of grace to you (John 1:16; 2 Pet. 1:4). I am the God of hope (Rom. 15:13), the God of love (2 Cor. 13:11), the God of patience (Rom. 15:5), the author and finisher of faith (Heb. 12:2), the God of all grace (1 Pet. 5:10), and I will give grace to you (Psa. 84:11). My design is to make you partakers of my holiness (Heb. 12:10). I will be a constant spring of spiritual life to you (Gal. 2:20; John 14; 8:12; 10:10). The water that I shall give you, shall be in you as a well of water, springing up into everlasting life (John 4:14). The seed of life that I shall put into you, shall be so fed, and cherished, and maintained by my power, that it shall be immortal (1 John 3:9; 1 Pet. 1:23; Col. 2:19). The unction that you shall receive from the Holy One, shall abide in you, and teach you all things necessary for you, and as it has taught you, you shall abide in him (John 14:16, 17; 1 John 2:20, 27). Keep but the pipes open, and ply the means which I have prescribed, and you shall flourish in the courts of your God (Prov. 8:34; Psa. 92:13). Yes, I will satisfy your souls in drought, and make fat your bones, and you shall be like a watered garden. Lo, I will be as the dew to you, and you shall grow as the lily, and cast forth your roots as Lebanon; and your branches shall spread, and your beauty shall be as the olive tree (Hos. 14:5, 6). You shall still bring forth fruit in old age, you shall be fat and flourishing.

His sovereignty to be (as it were) commanded by us.

My *sovereignty* shall be commanded by you (Gen. 32:26, 28; Deut. 9:14). You shall be my favourites, men of power, to prevail with me (Hos. 12:4; James 5:17, 18). All my attributes shall be at the command of your prayers (Isa. 45:11).

His all-sufficiency to be the lot of our inheritance.

In sum, my *all-sufficiency* shall be the lot of your inheritance (Gen. 17:1; Lam. 3:24; Psa. 16:5, 6). My fulness is your treasure (Num. 18:20; Deut. 10:9). My house is your home (Psa. 91:1, 9). You may come as freely to my store as to your own cupboard (Eph. 3:12). You may have your hand as freely in my treasures as in your own purses. You cannot ask too much, you cannot look for too much from me (Eph. 3:20; Matt. 7:8). I will give you, or be myself to you instead of, all comforts (Gen. 15:1; Psa. 84:11). You shall have children, or I will be better to you than ten children (Isa. 56:5). You shall have riches, or I will be more to you than all riches (2 Cor. 6:10).

You shall have friends, if best for you, or else I will be your comforter in your solitude (Isa. 51:3; John 14:26; 2 Cor. 1:3, 4), your counsellor in your distress (Psa. 73:24). If you leave father or mother, or houses or lands, for my sake, you shall have a hundred-fold in me, even in this time (Mark 10:30). When your enemies shall remove your comforts, it shall be but as the letting the cistern run, and opening the fountain, or putting out the candles, and letting in the sun. The swelling of the waters shall raise higher the ark of your comfort (Rom. 5:3; Heb. 10:34; Acts 5:41). I will be the staff of bread to you, your life, and the strength of your days (Deut. 30:20; Isa. 33:16). I will be the house and home to you, you shall dwell with me; yes, dwell in me and I in you (Deut. 33:12; John 14:23; 1 John 3:24). I will stand and fall with you (Psa. 37:17, 24; 54:4; Isa. 41:10). I will repair your losses, and relieve your needs (Phil. 4:19; Mark 8:35; Matt. 19:27-29). Can you burn out the lamp of heaven, or ladle out the boundless ocean with your hands? Why, the sun shall be dark, and the sea be dry, before the Father of lights, the Fountain of mercies shall be exhausted. Behold, though the world has been spending upon the stock of my mercy, ever since I created man upon earth, yet it runs with full stream still. My sun diffuses its rays and disburses its light, and yet shines as bright as ever: much more can I dispense of my goodness, and fill my creatures brimful, and running over, and yet have never the less in myself: and till this all-sufficiency be spent, you shall never be undone. I am the God of Abraham, and of Isaac, and of Jacob, and whatever I was to them, I will be to you.

Are you in want? You know where to go. I am ever at home; you shall not go away empty from my door. Never distract yourselves with cares and fears, but make known your requests by prayer and supplication to me (Phil. 4:6). I will help when all else fails (Psa. 73:26; Isa. 63:5; Psa. 102:17). When friends fail, and hearts fail; when your eyestrings crack and your heartstrings crack; when your acquaintances leave you, and your souls leave you, my bosom shall be open to you (Psa. 49:15; 2 Cor. 5:1; Luke 16:22). I will lock up your dust, I will receive your souls.

His infiniteness to be the extent of our inheritance.

And my *infiniteness* shall be the extent of your inheritance. Can you by searching find out God? can you find out the Almighty to perfection? it is high as heaven, what can you do? deeper than hell, what can you know? (Job 11:7, 8). This height incomprehensible, this deep unfathomable, shall be all yours, for ever yours.

I am your inheritance which no line can measure, no arithmetic can value, no surveyor can describe (Ezek. 44:28; Eph. 3:8; 1 Tim. 6:16; Psa. 145:3).

Lift up now your eyes to the ancient mountains, and to the utmost bounds of the everlasting hills. All that you can see is yours: but your short sight cannot know the half of what I give you: and when you see and know most, you are no less than infinitely short of the discovery of your own riches (Job 26:14).

(2) *In all his personal relations.*

Yea, further, I will be yours in all my *personal relations.*

God the Father to be a Father to us.

I am the everlasting Father, and I will be *a Father* to you (John 20:17). I take you for my sons and daughters (2 Cor. 6:18). Behold, I receive you not as servants, but as sons to abide in my house forever (John 8:35, 36). Whatever love or care children may look for from their father, that may you expect from me (Matt. 6:31, 32); and so much more as I am wiser, and greater, and better than any earthly parent. If earthly fathers will give good things to their children, much more will I give to you (Luke 11:13). If such cannot forget their children, much less will I forget you (Isa. 49:15). What would my children have? Your Father's heart, and your Father's house (Job 7:17; John 14:2); your Father's care, and your Father's ear; your Father's bread (1 Pet. 5:7; Matt. 7:9), and your Father's rod (Heb. 12:7); these shall be all yours.

He promises his fatherly affections.

You shall have my fatherly *affection*; my heart I share among you, my tenderest love I bestow upon you (1 John 3:1; Jer. 31:3; Isa. 54:8).

His fatherly compassion.

My fatherly *compassion*. As a father pities his children, so will I pity you (Psa. 103:13, 14). I will consider your frame, and not be extreme to mark what is done amiss by you, but cover all with the mantle of my excusing love (Psa. 78:38).

His fatherly instruction.

My fatherly *instruction*. I will cause you to hear the sweet voice behind you saying, This is the way (Isa. 30:21). I will be tender towards your weakness, and inculcate my admonitions, line upon line, and feed you with milk when you cannot digest stronger meat (Isa. 28:13; 1 Cor. 3:2). I will instruct you, and guide you with my eye (Psa. 32:8).

His fatherly protection.

My fatherly *protection*. In my fear is strong confidence, and my children shall have a place of refuge (Prov. 14:26). My name shall be your strong tower, to which you may at all times fly and be safe (Prov. 18:10). To your stronghold, you prisoners of hope (Zech. 9:12). I am an open refuge, a near and inviolable refuge for you (Psa. 48:3; Deut. 4:7; John 10:29).

His fatherly provision.

My fatherly *provision*. Be not afraid of want; in your Father's house there is bread enough (Psa. 34:9; Luke 15:17). I will care for your bodies. Do not worry about what you shall eat, drink, or put on. Let it suffice you, that your heavenly Father knows that you have need of all things (Matt. 6:25-34; Luke 12:22-32). I will provide for your souls, meat for them, and mansions for them, and portions for them (John 6:30-59; Lam. 3:24).

Behold, I have spread the table of my gospel for you, with privileges and comforts that no man takes from you (Isa. 25:6; Matt. 22:4; Prov. 9:2). I have set before you the bread of life, and the tree of life, and the water of life (John 6:48; Rev. 2:7; 22:17). Eat, O friends; drink abundantly, O beloved.

But all this is but a taste of what I have prepared. You must have but smiles and hints now, and be contented with glimpses and glances here; but you shall be shortly taken up into your Father's bosom, and live for ever in the fullest views of his glory (1 Thess. 4:17).

His fatherly probation.

My fatherly *probation.* I will chasten you because I love you, that you may not be condemned with the world (1 Cor. 11:32; Prov. 3:11, 12).

God the Son to be a Husband to us.

My Son I give to you, in a marriage-covenant for ever (Isa. 9:6; 42:6; 2 Cor. 11:2). I make him over to you as wisdom, for your illumination; righteousness, for your justification; sanctification, for the curing of your corruptions; redemption, for your deliverance from your enemies (1 Cor. 1:30). I bestow him upon you with all his fulness, all his merits, and all his graces. He shall be yours in all his offices.

I have anointed him for a *Prophet.* Are you ignorant, he shall teach you; he shall be eyesalve to you (Isa. 49:6; 42:16; Rev. 3:18); I have sent him to preach the gospel to the poor, and recovering of sight to the blind; to set at liberty those who are bruised (Luke 4:18).

I have established him by oath, as a *Priest* for ever (Psa. 110:4). If any sin, he shall be your Advocate: he shall expiate your guilt, and make the atonement (1 John 2:1, 2; Zech. 13:1). Have you any sacrifice, any service to offer, bring it to him, and you shall receive an answer of peace (1 Pet. 2:5; Heb. 13:15). Present your petitions by his hand, him will I accept (John 16:23, 24). Having such a High Priest over the house of God (Heb. 10:19-22), you may come and be welcome; come with boldness.

Him have I set up as *King* upon my holy hill of Zion. He shall rule you, he shall defend you (Isa. 9:6, 7). He is the King of righteousness, King of peace; and such a King shall he be to you (Heb. 7:2; Jer. 23:6; Eph. 2:14). I will set up his standard for you (Isa. 49:22); I will set up his throne in you (Psa. 110:2). He shall reign in righteousness, and rule in judgment; and he shall be a hiding-place from the wind, and a shelter from the tempest, and the shadow of a great rock in a weary land (Isa. 32:1, 2). He shall hear your causes, judge your enemies (Isa. 11:3-5), and reign till he has put all under his feet (Psa. 110:1; 1 Cor. 15:25); yes, and under your feet; for they shall be as ashes under you, and you shall tread them, says the Lord of hosts (Mal. 4:3). Yes, I will undo those who afflict you, and all those who despised you shall bow themselves down at the soles of your feet (Zeph. 3:19; Isa. 60:14). And you shall go forth and behold the carcasses of the men who have trespassed against me, for their worm shall not die, neither shall their fire be quenched; and they shall be abhorrent to all flesh (Isa. 66:24).

God the Spirit to be Counsellor and Comforter to us.

My Spirit I give to you for your Counsellor and your Comforter (John 16:7; Rom. 8:14). He shall be a constant inmate with you, and shall dwell in you and abide with you forever (Ezek. 36:27; John 14:16, 17).

I consecrate you as temples to his holiness (1 Cor. 3:16, 17; 6:19). He shall be your guide, he shall lead you into all truth (Gal. 5:18; John 16:13). He shall be your advocate to indite your prayers, and make intercession for you, and shall fill your mouths with the arguments that he knows will prevail with me (Rom. 8:26, 27). He shall be oil to your wheels, and strength to your ankles, wine to your hearts, and marrow to your bones, and wind to your sails. He shall witness your adoption (Rom. 8:16). He shall seal you up to the day of redemption, and be to you the deposit which guarantees your inheritance, until the redemption of the purchased possession (Eph. 4:30; 1:13, 14; 2 Cor. 1:22).

2. *He gives with himself all things both present and to come.*

And as I give you myself, so much more all things with myself (Rom. 8:32). Earth and heaven, life and death, *things present* and *things to come* (1 Cor. 3:22).

(1) *Things present ours.*

Things present are yours; lo, I give you Caleb's blessing, the upper springs and the lower springs. I will bless you with all spiritual blessings in heavenly places in Christ (Eph. 1:3).

(i) *The 'upper springs' or blessings spiritual, as adoption, access, audience, peace, perseverance, etc.*

To you pertains the adoption, and the glory, and the covenants, and the service of God, and the promises (Rom. 9:4). To you I will give the white stone, and the new name (Rev. 2:17), access into my presence (Eph. 3:12), the acceptance of your persons (Eph. 1:6), the audience of your prayers (1 John 5:14, 15).

Peace I leave with you, my peace I give to you (John 14:27). I will undertake for your perseverence, and keep you to the end, and then will crown my own gift with eternal life (Jer. 32:40; John 10:28, 29; 1 Pet. 1:5; Phil. 1:6). I have made you heirs of God, and co-heirs with your Lord Jesus Christ, and you shall inherit all things (Rom. 8:17; Rev. 21:7).

The protection of his angels.

I have granted you my angels for your guardians. The courtiers of heaven shall attend to you; they shall be all ministering spirits for your good (Heb. 1:14). Behold, I have given them charge over you, upon their fidelity to look after you, and, as the tender nurses, to bear you in their arms, and to keep you from coming to any hurt (Psa. 91:11, 12). These shall be as the careful shepherds, to watch over my flock by night, and to encamp round about my fold (Psa. 34:7).

The oversight of his ministers.

My ministers I give for your guides (Eph. 4:11). Paul, Apollos, Cephas, all are yours (1 Cor. 3:22). I am always with them, and they shall be always with you, to the end of the world (Matt. 28:20; Eph. 4:13). You shall have pastors after my own heart (Jer. 3:15; 23:4), and this shall be my covenant with you, that my Spirit which is upon you, and my words which I have put into your mouth, shall not depart out of your mouth, nor the mouth of your seed, nor of your seed's seed, says the Lord, from this time forth and for ever (Isa. 59:21).

The rod of his discipline.

In short, all my officers shall be for the profiting and perfecting of you (Eph. 4:12). All my ordinances shall be for edifying and saving you (Acts 10:33; Rom. 1:16). The very severities of my house, admonitions, censures, *etc.* and the whole discipline of my family, shall be for preventing your infection, curing corruption, procuring your salvation (1 Cor. 5:5-7; Matt. 18:15).

My word have I ordained for converting your soul, enlightening your eyes, rejoicing your hearts, cautioning you of dangers, cleansing your defilements, and conforming you to my image (Psa. 19:7-9, 1; Eph. 5:26; 2 Cor. 3:18). To you I commit the oracles of God (Rom. 3:2). Here you shall be furnished against temptations (Matt. 4:4, 7; Eph. 6:17), hence you shall be comforted under distresses and afflictions (Psa. 119: 92, 93). Here you shall find my whole counsel (Acts 20:27). This shall instruct you in your way, correct you in your wanderings, direct you into the truths to be believed, detect to you the errors to be rejected (2 Tim. 3:16; Psa. 119:105).

The pledges of his sacraments.

My sacraments I give you, as the pledges of my love. You shall freely claim them, they are children's bread. Lo! I have given them as seals, to certify all that I have here promised you (Rom. 4:11); and when these sacred signs are delivered to you, then know, and remember, and consider in your hearts, that I therein plight you my troth,[2] and set to my hand, and do thereby ratify and confirm every article of these indentures,[3] and do actually deliver into your own hands this glorious charter, with all its immunities and privileges, as your own for ever (1 Cor. 11:25; Gen. 17:10).

(ii) *The 'lower springs' or mercies temporal.*

And having sowed to you so largely in spiritual blessings, shall you not much more reap *the temporal*? Do not be of doubtful mind, all these things shall be added to you (Luke 12:29, 31).

The supply of his creatures.

My creatures I grant for your servants and supplies (Psa. 8:3-9). Heaven and earth shall minister to you. All the stars in their courses shall serve you, and, if need be, shall fight for you (Judg. 5:20). And I will make my covenant for you with the beasts of the

---

[2] plight you my troth = pledge you my oath of fidelity (as in a marriage).
[3] indentures = binding legal documents.

field, and with the fowls of heaven; and you shall be in league with the stones of the field, and all shall be at peace with you (Job 5:23; Hos. 2:18). I will undertake for all your necessities. Do I feed the fowls, and clothe the grass, and do you think I will neglect my children? (Matt. 6:25-34). I hear the young ravens when they cry, shall I not much more fulfil the desires of those who fear me? (Psa. 145:19 with 147:9). Fear not, you shall be sure to lack no good thing (Psa. 34:10); and you would not yourselves desire riches, pleasures, or preferment, to your hurt. I will give food to them that fear me: I will be ever mindful of my covenant (Psa. 111:5).

The co-operation of his providences.

My providences shall co-operate to your good (Rom. 8:28). The cross winds shall blow you the sooner and swifter into your harbour. You shall be preferred, when you seem most debased; and then be greatest gainers, when you seem to be deepest losers, and most effectually promote your good, when you seem most to deny it (2 Cor. 4:17; Mark 10:29; Phil. 1:29).

(2) Things to come ours.

Things to come are yours, the perfecting of your souls, the redemption of your bodies, the consummation of your bliss.

At death in glorification initiate.

When you have glorified me for a while on earth, and finished the work I have given you to do, you shall be caught up into paradise, and rest from your labours, and your works shall follow you (Rev. 14:13; Luke 23:43).

The convoy of angels.

I will send of my own lifeguard, to conduct home your departing souls (Luke 16:22), and receive you among the spirits of just men made perfect (Heb. 12:23). And you shall look back upon Pharaoh, and all his host, and see your enemies dead upon the shore.

Redemption from all afflictions and corruptions.

Then shall be your redemption from all your afflictions, and all your corruptions (Luke 21:28; Eph. 4:30).

The thorn in the flesh taken out.

The thorn in the flesh shall be pulled out, and the hour of temptation shall be over, and the tempter for ever out of work.

The sweat wiped from off our brows.

The sweat shall be wiped off from your brows, and the day of cooling and refreshing shall come, and you shall sit down for ever under my shadow (Acts 3:19; Heb. 4:9). For the Lamb that is in the midst of the throne shall feed you, and lead you to the living fountains of water (Rev. 7:17).

The tears wiped away from our eyes.

The tears shall be wiped away from your eyes, and there shall be no more sorrow, nor crying, neither shall there be any more pain; for the former things are passed away, and behold I make all things new (Rev. 21:4, 5). I will change Marah into Naomi, and the cup of sorrow into the cup of salvation; and the bread and water of affliction into the wine of eternal consolation (John 16:20-22; Luke 6:21). You shall take down your harps from the willows, and I will turn your tears into pearls, and your penitential psalms into songs of deliverance. You shall change your Ichabods into hosannas, and your cries of sorrow into hallelujahs of joy (Rev. 19:1, 4, 6).

The cross taken off from our backs.

The cross shall be taken off from your backs, and you shall come out of your great tribulations, and wash your robes, and make them white in the blood of the Lamb, and you shall be before the throne of God, and serve him night and day in his temple, and he who sits on the throne shall dwell among you, and you shall hunger no more, and thirst no more, neither shall the sun light upon you, nor any heat (Rev. 7:14-16).

The load taken off from our consciences.

The load shall be taken off from your consciences. Sins and doubts shall no more defile you or distress you (Rev. 22:17; Heb. 12:23). I will make an end of sin, and knock off the fetters of your corruptions, and you shall be a glorious church, not having spot or wrinkle, or any such thing; but holy and without blemish (Eph. 5:27; Rev. 7:9, 13, 14).

The soul's admission into the chamber of the presence and vision of God.

Thus shall you be brought to the King all glorious, in robes interwoven with gold; with gladness and rejoicing shall you be brought, and enter into the King's palace (Psa. 45:9, 13-15). So shall the beloved of the Lord dwell safely by him, and you shall stand continually before him, and behold the beauty of the Lord, and hear his wisdom (1 Cor. 13:12). Then will I open in you an everlasting spring of joy, and you shall break forth into singing, and never cease more, nor rest day nor night, saying, Holy, holy, holy (Rev. 4:8; Psa. 16:11).

Thus shall the grand enemy expire with your breath, and the body of death be put off with your dying body; and the day of your death shall be the birthday of your glories (Phil. 1:23; Luke 23:43).

Have faith in God (Mark 11:22). Wait but a little, and sorrow shall cease, and sin be no more.

At the resurrection, in glorification consummate, redemption complete.

And then a little longer, and death shall be no more (Rev. 20:14; 21:4); but your last enemy shall be destroyed, and your victory completed. Yet a little while, and he that shall come, will come, and you also shall appear with him in glory (Heb. 10:37; Col. 3:4).

The return of the Redeemer.

This same Jesus which is taken from you into heaven, shall so come as he went up into heaven (Acts 1:11): and when he comes, he will receive you to himself, that where he is there you may be also (John 14:3). Behold his sign; he comes in the clouds of heaven with power and great glory; and every eye shall see him, and all the tribes of the earth shall mourn because of him (Rev. 1:7; Matt. 24:30), but you shall lift up your heads, because the day of your redemption draws near (Luke 21:28).

The rising of the body.

Then shall he sound his trumpet (1 Cor. 15:52; 1 Thess. 4:16), and make you hear his voice in your dust (John 5:28), and shall send his mighty angels to gather you from the four winds of heaven (Matt. 24:31), who shall carry you in the triumphant chariot of the clouds, to meet your Lord (1 Thess. 4:17); and you shall be prepared for him, and presented to him, as a bride adorned for her husband (Rev. 21:2).

Full conformity, both in body and soul, to our glorified Saviour.

And as you have borne the image of the earthly, so shall you bear the image of the heavenly; and you shall be fully conformed both in body and spirit to your glorious Head (Phil. 3:21; Heb. 12:2, 3).

Public approbation and absolution.

Then shall he confess you before his angels (Rev. 3:5), and you shall receive your open absolution before all flesh, and be owned, approved, and applauded in the public audience of the general assembly (Matt. 10:32; 25:32, 34, 35, etc.).

Solemn espousals.

And you shall be with all royal solemnities, espoused to the King of glory, in the presence of all his shining courtiers (Rev. 19:7, 8;

2 Cor. 4:14; Matt. 25:31), to the envy, and gnashing, and terror of your adversaries (Luke 13:28).

The coronation and enthronement of the saints. Their sitting in judgment upon the world.

So shall your Lord, with his own hand, crown you (Rev. 2:10), and set you on thrones (Rev. 3:21; Matt. 19:28), and you shall judge men and angels (1 Cor. 6:2, 3), and you shall have power over the nations (Rev. 2:26, 27), and you shall set your feet upon the necks of your enemies (Psa. 18:40).

Lo, I have set the very day for your instalment (Acts 17:31), I have provided your crowns (2 Tim. 4:8), I have prepared the kingdom (Matt. 25:34). Why do you doubt, O you of little faith? these are the true sayings of God (Rev. 19:9). Are you sure that you are now on earth? so surely shall you be shortly with me in heaven. Are you sure that you shall die? so surely shall you rise again in glory. Lo, I have said it, and who shall reverse it? You shall see me face to face, and be with me where I am, and behold my glory (1 Cor. 13:12; John 17:24). For I will be glorified in my saints, and admired in all them that believe (2 Thess. 1:10); and all flesh shall know that I have loved you (Rev. 3:9). For I will make you the instances of my grace (Eph. 1:5, 6; 2:7), in whom the whole world shall see how unutterably the Almighty God can advance the poor worm's meat, and dust of the ground. And the despisers shall behold, and wonder, and perish (Acts 13:41): for they shall be witnesses to the riches of my magnificence, and the exceeding greatness of my power (Luke 16:23). They shall go away into everlasting punishment, but you into life eternal (Matt. 25:46).

Our triumphant ascension into heaven.

For no sooner shall their doom be passed, but the bench shall rise (Matt. 25:41, 46), and the Judge shall return with all his glorious train; with sound of trumpet and shouts incredible shall he ascend, and shall lead you to your Father's house (Psa. 45:14, 15; Matt. 25:23; John 14:2 with 2 Cor. 5:1). Then shall the triumphal arches lift up their heads, and the everlasting gates stand open, and the heavens shall receive you all, and so shall you be ever with the Lord (John 12:26; 1 Thess. 4:17).

And now will I rejoice over you with singing, and rest in my love; and heaven shall ring with joys and acclamations, because I have received you safe and sound (Luke 15:20, 23, 25, 27).

Blessed eternity.

And in that day you shall know that I am a rewarder of them that diligently seek me (Heb. 11:6); and that I did record your words (Mal. 3:16), and bottle your tears, and tell your wanderings (Psa. 56:8), and keep an account, even to a cup of cold water, of whatever you said or did for my name (Matt. 10:42). You shall surely find that nothing is lost (1 Cor. 15:58); but you shall have full measure, pressed down and running over, thousands of years in paradise, for the least good thought, and thousand thousands for the least good word; and then the reckoning shall begin again, till all arithmetic be at a loss. For you shall be swallowed up in a blessed eternity, and the doors of heaven shall be shut upon you, and there shall be no more going out (Dan. 12:2, 3; Rev. 3:12; Luke 16:26).

Glorious company.

The glorious choir of my holy angels, the goodly fellowship of my blessed prophets, the happy society of triumphant apostles, the royal hosts of victorious martyrs, these shall be your companions for ever (Matt. 8:11, 12; Heb. 12:22, 23). And you shall come in white robes, with palms in your hands, everyone having the harps of God, and golden bowls full of sweet-smelling aromas, and shall cast your crowns before me, and strike in with the multitude of the heavenly hosts, glorifying God, and saying, Hallelujah! the Lord

God omnipotent reigns (Rev. 7:9-12; 19:5, 6). Blessing, honour, glory, and power be to him who sits on the throne, and to the Lamb for ever and ever (Rev. 5:13).

Beatifical vision.

In short, I will make you equal to the angels of God (Luke 20:36), and you shall be the everlasting trumpets of my praise (Rev. 7:10-12, 15). You shall be abundantly satisfied with the fatness of my house, and I will make you drink of the rivers of my pleasures (Psa. 36:8). You shall be an eternal excellency (Isa. 60:15), and if God can die, and eternity run out, then and only then, shall your joys expire. For you shall see me as I am (1 John 3:2), and know me as you are known (1 Cor. 13:12); and shall behold my face in righteousness, and be satisfied with my likeness (Psa. 17:15). And you shall be the vessels of my glory, whose blessed use shall be to receive the overflowings of my goodness, and to have mine infinite love and glory poured out into you brimful, and running over for evermore (Rom. 9:23; 2 Tim 2:20; Rev. 22:1).

And blessed is he who has believed, for there shall be a performance of the things that have been told him (Luke 1:45). I the Lord has spoken it, you shall see my face, and my name shall be written in your foreheads; and you shall no more need the sun, nor the moon, for the Lord God shall give you light, and you shall reign for ever and ever (Rev. 22:3-5).

(3) *He takes us for his people.*

And as I give myself to you for your God, and all things with myself; so *I take you for my covenant people* (Heb. 8:10; Isa. 43:1), and you shall be mine in the day when I make up my jewels, says the Lord of hosts; and I will spare you as a man spares his own son who serves him (Mal. 3:17). The Lord shall count when he writes up the people, Surely they are my children (Psa. 87:6).

I do not only require you to be mine, if you would have me to be for you; but I do promise to make you mine (Lev. 20:26; Ezek. 36:28), and to work in you the conditions which I require of you. I will circumcise your hearts to love me (Deut. 30:6). I will take out the heart of stone (Ezek. 36:26). My laws I will write within you (Jer. 31:33).

Yet you must know that I will be sought after for these things (Ezek. 36:37), and as ever you expect to partake of the mercies, I charge you to lie at the pool, and wait for my Spirit, and be diligent in the use of the means (Prov. 2:3-5; 8:34; Luke 11:13).

I am content to abate the rigour of the old terms (Rom. 4:6); I shall not stand upon satisfaction (Luke 7:42). I have received a ransom, and do only expect your acceptance (Rev. 22:17; 1 Tim. 2:6). I shall not insist upon perfection (1 John 1:8, 9). Walk before me, and be upright, and sincerity shall carry the crown (Prov. 11:20; Gen. 17:1; Psa. 97:11). Yes, both the faith and obedience that I require of you are my own gifts (Eph. 2:8).

I require you to accept my Son by believing: but I will give you a hand to take him (Phil. 1:29; John 6:65), and to submit to, and obey him: but I must and will guide your hand to write after him, and cause you to walk in my statutes (Ezek. 36:27). I will take you by the arms, and teach you to go (Hos. 11:3, 4): I will order your steps (Psa. 37:23, 31). Yea, those things will I accept of you as the conditions of life, which, viewed in the strictness of my justice, would deserve eternal death (Eph. 3:8 with 1 Thess. 3:10; Heb. 5:5, 9 with Eccles. 7:20). Grace! Grace!

The Voice of the Redeemed

Amen, hallelujah. May it be to your servants according to your word. But who are we, and what is our father's house, that you have brought us thus far? And now, O Lord God, what shall your servants say to you? for we are silenced with wonder, and must sit down in astonishment, for we cannot utter the least syllable of your praises. What is the meaning of the height of this strange love? And why is it shown to us, that the Lord of heaven and earth should condescend to enter into covenant with his dust, and take into his bosom the viperous brood that has so often spat its venom in his face? We are not worthy to be as the handmaids, to wash the feet of the servants of our Lord: how much less to be your sons and heirs, and to be made partakers of all these blessed liberties and privileges which you have settled upon us! But for your goodness' sake, and according to your own heart, have you done all these great things. Even so, Father, because so it seemed good in your sight.

For this reason you are great, O God, for there is none like you, neither is there any God besides you. And what nation on earth is like your people, whom God redeemed to be a people for himself, and to make a name for himself, and to do for them great and awesome things? For you have confirmed them to yourself, that they are a people for yourself forever, and you, Lord, have become their God to the end (2 Sam. 7:18).

Wonder, O heavens, and be moved, O earth, at this great thing! (Rev. 21:4). For behold, the tabernacle of God is with men, and he will dwell with them, and they shall be his people, and God himself shall be with them, and be their God. Be astonished and ravished with wonder, for the infinite breach is made up; the offender is received, God and man reconciled, and a covenant of peace entered, and heaven and earth are all agreed upon the terms, and have struck their hands, and sealed the indentures. O happy conclusion! O blessed conjunction! Shall the stars dwell with the dust? or the wide distant poles be brought to mutual embraces?

But here the distance of the terms is infinitely greater. Rejoice, O angels! shout, O seraphim! O all you friends of the Bridegroom, prepare a wedding song, be ready with the marriage song! Lo, here is the wonder of wonders: for Jehovah has betrothed himself for ever to his hopeless captives, and owns the marriage before all the world, and is become one with us, and we with him. He has bequeathed to us the precious things of heaven above, and the precious things of the earth beneath, with its fullness, and has kept back nothing from us.

And now, O Lord, you are that God, and your words are true, and you have promised this goodness to your servants, and has left us nothing to ask at your hands but what you have already freely granted. Only the word which you have spoken concerning your servants, establish it for ever, and do as you have said, and let your name be magnified for ever, saying, The Lord of hosts, he is the God of Israel. Amen. Hallelujah.

END OF PART ONE.

PART TWO

TRIUMPH IN THE COVENANT,

OR,

A SOLILOQUY,

REPRESENTING THE BELIEVER'S TRIUMPH IN GOD'S COVENANT; AND THE VARIOUS CONFLICTS AND GLORIOUS CONQUESTS OF FAITH OVER UNBELIEF.

The soul takes hold of God's covenant.

Yes, has God said, I will be your God? Is it true indeed? Will the Lord be mine? Will he lay aside the controversy, and conclude a peace? Will he receive the rebel to mercy, and open his doors to his prodigal? I will surely go to my Father; I will take with me words, and bow myself before his footstool, and say, O Lord, I have heard your words, and do here lay hold of your covenant (Isa. 56:4). I accept the kindness of God, and will adventure myself upon your fidelity, and trust my whole happiness here and hereafter upon these your promises.

Farewell, deceitful world, get yourself under my feet. Too long have I feared your vain threats; too long have I been deluded with your flattering promises. Can you promise me or deny me such things as God has covenanted to give me? I know you cannot, and therefore I renounce you forever from being the object of my faith or fear. Nor longer will I lean on this rotten reed, no longer will I trust this broken idol. Avoid, Satan, with your tempting baits. In vain do you dress the harlot in her paint and bravery; and tell me, All this will I give you (Matt. 4:8, 9). Can you show me such a crown, such a kingdom as God has promised to settle on me? Or that which will balance the loss of an infinite God, who here gives himself to me? Away deceitful lusts and pleasures, get away from me; I have enough in Christ and in his promise to give my soul full contentment; these have I lodged in my heart, and there is no longer room for such guests as you. Never again shall you have quiet entertainment within these doors.

God of truth, I here take you at your word; you require only my acceptance and consent, and here you have it. Good is the word of the Lord which he has spoken, and as my Lord has said, so will your servant do. My soul catches hold of your promises. These have I taken as my inheritance for ever. Let others carry the preferments and possessions of this world, it shall be enough for me to be an heir of your promises.

She makes her boast in God.

O happy soul, how rich are you! What a booty have I gotten! It is all my own. I have the promises of this life, and of that which is to come (1 Tim. 4:8). O what more can I wish for! How full a charter is here! Now my doubting soul may boldly and believingly say with Thomas, My Lord, and my God! What need do we have of any further witness? We have heard his words. He has sworn by his holiness that his decree may not be changed, and has signed it with his own signet.

Rejoice, you heavens; strike up, you celestial choirs. Help heaven and earth. Sing to the Lord, O you saints of his. Bless the Lord, O my soul. O had I the tongues of men and angels, all were too little for my single turn. Had I as many tongues as hairs, the whole were not sufficient to utter my Creator's praises.

My beloved is mine, and I am his (Song of Sol. 2:16). The grant is clear, and my claim is firm. Who dares deny it, when God himself owns it? Is it a hard task to speak after Christ himself? Why, this is the message that he has sent me: I ascend to my Father and your Father, my God and your God (John 20:17). He has put words into my mouth, and bid me say, Our Father.

I believe; Lord, help my unbelief. O my God, and my Father, I accept you with all humble thankfulness, and am bold to take hold of you. O my King and my God, I subject my soul and all its powers to you. O my glory, in you will I boast all the day. O my rock, on you will I build all my confidence and my hopes. O staff of my life, and strength of my heart; the life of my joys, and joy of my life; I will sit and sing under your shadow, and glory in your holy name (Song of Sol. 2:3).

O my soul, arise and take possession. Inherit your blessedness, and cast up your riches. Yours is the kingdom, yours is the glory, and yours is the victory. The whole Trinity is yours. All the persons in the Godhead, all the attributes in the Godhead are yours. And behold, here is the evidence, and these are the writings, by which all is made sure to you for ever.

She quells discontentment and reasons down unbelief.

And now, Return to your rest, O my soul; for the Lord has dealt bountifully with you (Psa. 116:7). Say if your lines have not fallen to you in a pleasant place, and if this is not a good inheritance! (Psa. 16:6). O blasphemous discontent! how absurd and unreasonable an evil are you, whom all the fulness of the Godhead cannot satisfy, because you are denied in a petty comfort, or crossed in your vain expectations from the world? O my unthankful soul, shall not a Trinity content you? Shall not all-sufficiency suffice you? Silence, you murmuring thoughts, for ever. I have enough, I abound, and am full. Infiniteness and eternity are mine, and what more can I ask?

The assaults of unbelief and the responses of faith.

1. Unbelief questions the truth of the promises.

But I think I feel some secret checks upon my joy, and when I would soar aloft, and triumph in the riches of my portion, a secret diffidence plucks me back, as the string does the bird, and unbelief whispers in my ear, Surely this is too good to be true?

But who are you who disputes against God? The Lord has spoken it, and shall I not believe him? Will he be angry if I give my assent, and speak it confidently upon the credit of his words?

Faith triumphs in the certainty of God's truth.

O my Lord, suffer me to spread the writing before you. Have you not said, Your Maker is your husband? (Isa. 54:5). I will betroth you to me? (Hos. 2:19). You shall call me, My father? (Jer. 3:19). I pray you, O Lord, was not this your saying, I am God, even your God? (Psa. 50:7). I will be a Father to you, and you my sons and daughters? (2 Cor. 6:18). Why then should I doubt? Is not the truth of the living God a sure footing for my faith?

Silence then, O quarrelling unbelief. I know in whom I have believed. Not in friends, though numerous and potent; for they are men, and not God (Isa. 31:3). Not in riches, for they make themselves wings (Prov. 23:5). Not in princes, for their breath is in their nostrils (Psa. 146:3, 4). But let God be true, and every man a liar. In God have I put my trust, in his word do I hope. O sure word! Heaven and earth shall pass away, but not one jot or tittle of this; I have not built upon the sand of mortality. Let the rain descend, and the floods come, and the winds blow, nevertheless the foundation of God stands sure. His everlasting counsel and everlasting covenant are my support. I am built upon his promises, and let hell and earth do their worst to blow up this foundation (Matt. 7:25; 2 Tim. 2:19).

Now shall my faith triumph, and my heart be glad, and my glory rejoice. I will shout with the exulting multitude. The Lord he is the God (1 Kings 18:39), and he is not ashamed to be called my God (Heb. 11:16). He is not ashamed of my rags or poverty, of my parentage or pedigree; and since his infinite condescension will own me, will he take it ill if I own him? Though I have nothing of my own to glory in (1 Cor. 1:29, 31), (unless I should glory in my shame) yet I will glory in the Lord, and bless myself in him.

For who is like the God of Jeshurun? (Deut. 33:26). Bring forth your gods, O you nations. Lift up your eyes, and behold who has created all these things. Can any do for their favourites as the Lord can? Or if he be angry, who is the god who shall deliver out of his hands? Will you set Dagon before the ark? Or shall Mammon contend with the Holy One? O ambitious Haman, where is now your idol honour? O rich glutton, who made a god of pleasure, where is now the god whom you have served? O sensual worldling, who knew not where nor how to give away your goods: do riches profit you? Could Mammon save you? Deceived souls! go now to the gods whom you have chosen. Alas, they cannot for ever administer a drop of water to cool your tongues.

But the Portion of Jacob is not like them (Jer. 10:16). From everlasting to everlasting he is God (Psa. 90:2). His power is my confidence, his goodness is my maintenance, his truth is my shield and my buckler.

2. *Unbelief confounds the soul with the amazing greatness and difficulty of the things.*

But, my clamourous unbelief has many wiles, and afresh assaults me with the difficulty of the things promised, and labours to perplex and confound me with their amazing greatness.

Faith triumphs in God's omnipotency and veracity.

But why should I stagger at the promise through unbelief, robbing at once my Master of his glory, and my soul of her comfort?

It is my great sin to doubt and dispute, and yet shall I be afraid to believe? O my soul, it is the highest honour you can put upon your Lord, to believe against difficulties, and to look for and reckon upon great and wonderful things, passing all created power and human faith.

Let not the greatness, nor the strangeness of the benefits bequeathed to you, bring you to a halt. It is with a God you have to do, and therefore you must not look for little things; that were to darken the glory of his munificence, and the infiniteness of his power and goodness. Do you not know that it is his design to make his name glorious; and to make you know he is able to do for you above all you can ask or think? Surely they cannot be any small or ordinary things that shall be done for you, when the Lord shall show in you what a God can do, and shall carry you in triumph before the world, and make proclamation before you, Thus shall it be done to the man whom the Lord delights to honour. What wonder if you cannot comprehend these things?—if they exceed all your apprehensions and conceptions? This is a good argument for your faith: for this is that which the Lord has said, that it has not entered into the heart of man to conceive what things he has prepared for them that love him. Now if you could conceive and comprehend them, how should his word be made good? It is enough for you that the Lord has spoken it. Is not the word near you? Has God said, I will receive you? You shall be kings and priests unto God, and inherit all things; and shall sit on thrones, and judge angels, and be ever with the Lord, and shall I dare to say no to him? Unreasonable unbelief! What! never satisfied! still contradicting and blaspheming! False whisperer! no more of your tales. I believe God that it shall be as he has told me (Acts 27:25).

And now, thanks be to God, who always causes us to triumph in Christ (2 Cor. 2:14), therefore my lips shall praise you, and my soul which you have redeemed (Psa. 71:23). For you have made me glad through your word, and I will triumph in the works of your hands (Psa. 92:4). I will praise the Lord while I live. I will sing praises to my God while I have any being (Psa. 104:33).

O my soul, if you could wear out your fingers upon the harp, and wear your tongue to the roots, you could yet never sufficiently praise your Redeemer.

O my enemies! where is now your confidence, and where is your armour in which you trusted? I will set Christ alone against all your multitudes, and all the powers, and malice, and policy, with which they are armed. The field is already won, and the Captain of our salvation returned with the spoils of his enemies, having made a show of them openly, triumphing over them in his cross (Col. 2:15). And thanks be to God who has given us the victory through our Lord Jesus Christ (1 Cor. 15:57).

Of whom, then, should I be afraid? Behold he is near who justifies me; who shall plead with me?

O you powers of hell! you are but chained captives, and we have a sure word, that the gates of hell shall not prevail against us (Matt. 16:18). Though the world be in arms against us, and the devil at the head of them as their champion; yet who is this uncircumcised Philistine, that he should defy the armies of the living God? (1 Sam. 17:45-47). Behold, I have come out to you, as the stripling against Goliath; not with sword, and with spear, but in the name of the Lord of hosts, in whose strength I am more than a conqueror.

O grave, where is now your victory? Christ is risen, and has broken up your prison, and rolled away the stone, so that all your prisoners have made an escape. Rejoice not against me, O my enemy; though I fall, I shall rise again; though I lie in darkness, the Lord shall be a light unto me (Mic. 7:8). Enlarge not your desires, Tophet, but shut up your flaming mouth; for there is now no condemnation to those who are in Christ Jesus (Rom. 8:1).

O deceitful world, you are already overcome (John 16:33), and the conquered enemy has become my servant (1 Cor. 3:22), and I am fed with the honey taken out of the carcass of the slain lion. I fear not your threats, nor the enchantments of your siren songs, being kept by the power of God, through a victorious faith, for salvation (1 Pet. 1:5; 1 John 5:4).

O my sins, you are already buried, never to have any resurrection, and the remembrance of you shall be no more (Heb. 8:12). I see my sins nailed to the cross, and their dominion is taken away, though their lives be prolonged yet for a little season. Awake therefore, O my glory; awake psaltery and harp, and meet the deliverer with triumph; for his right hand, and his holy arm, have gotten us the victory (Psa. 98:1, 2), and all the ends of the earth have seen the salvation of our God.

3. *Unbelief upbraids the trembling soul with its unworthiness.*

Yet I think my unworthiness flies in my face, and I hear my cavilling unbelief thus upbraiding me, and crying out, O proud presumption! that you who are conscious to yourself of your great unworthiness, should pretend a claim to God and glory! Shall daring dust think to share with the Almighty, and say of his endless perfections, They are my right? Bold sinner, stand off, and tremble at your presumptuous arrogance.

Faith owns the charge, and triumphs in God's free grace.

O my God, I lay my hand upon my mouth. I confess the charge of my unworthiness. My guilt and shame is such as I cannot cover, but you can, and do. You have thrown a cloak over my nakedness, and have promised my transgressions shall not be mentioned, and that you will multiply pardons. And shall I take up what you have buried, and then frighten myself with the ghosts that infidelity has raised? Is it presumption to take the pardon that you offer? or to receive and claim you as mine, when it is but what you have promised? I dared not to have approached you, but upon your call; nor to have claimed to a title, but upon your grant. I should have thought it diabolical pride, to have pleaded an interest in you, and claimed kindred to you, but that you have shown me the way.

And you, my soul, are you ignorant of God's great design? Do you not know that it is his purpose to glorify free grace? And how should grace appear to be grace indeed, were there any worthiness in the subject? Your unworthiness is but a foil to set off the beauty and riches of free grace and mercy.

4. *Unbelief questions the believer's title to God's grace and interest in the promise.*

But I cannot shake off this brier: alas, what a cavilling sophister is unbelief! and will never be answered. Now is it ready to tell me, What if the promise should be a sure foundation! yet you may not build upon another man's ground. What though the grace and mercies of God are infinite! yet dogs may not catch at the children's bread. You have no right nor title to the promise, therefore cease your pretended claim.

Faith triumphs in the clearness of the believer's evidences.

But, O my soul, why should you doubt? Whose image and superscription is this? Do you not bear upon you the marks of the Lord Jesus? I have given up my name to him, and taken hold of his covenant (Isa. 56:4), and therefore may claim an interest.

I have accepted the matter, and closed with the Mediator, and subscribed to the conditions of the covenant, and therefore cannot question but it is mine.

The Lord has offered to be my God, and I have taken hold of his offer. I have taken him as God, and given him the supremacy. O my soul, look round about you, in heaven and in earth; is there any you esteem or value in comparison of God? (Psa. 73:25, 26). Is there any you love like him, or take that contentment or felicity in, which you do in him? (Phil. 3:8). Are not your chief desires and designs to glorify and enjoy him? (Phil. 1:20). You cannot deny, but it is truly thus. I am sure nothing but God will content me. I am never so well in all the world as in his company (Psa. 26:8; 84:1-3; 27:4). My soul seeks him above all, and rests in him alone, as my satisfactory portion (Psa. 119:57). He offers to take me as one of his people, and I have resigned myself accordingly to him as his, and have put both my inward and outward man under his government, and given up all to his disposal, and am resolved to be content with him, as my all-sufficient happiness (Psa. 119:38; 2 Cor. 5:8; Acts 24:16 with Rom. 6:19; Luke 14:33; Psa. 16:5, 6; John 1:12).

Besides, I have taken him in his own way through Christ, whom he has tendered to me as my head and husband, and I have accordingly, solemnly and deliberately taken him. O my soul, do you not know your frequent debates? (Luke 14:26-35). Have you not put Christ, and all the world, into the balance? Have you not cast up the cost, and reckoned upon the cross, and willingly put your neck under Christ's yoke (Matt. 11:29), and ventured your salvation upon Christ alone (Phil. 3:9), and trusted him with all your happiness, and all your hopes? (2 Tim. 1:12). Have you not over and over resolved to take him with what comes, and that he shall be enough, though in the loss of all things? (1 Cor. 1:30). You cannot but know, that these have been the transactions between Christ and you, and therefore he is yours, and all the promises, Yes and Amen to you through him.

And for the terms of the covenant, I love and like them; my soul embraces them; neither do I desire to be saved in any other way, than by repentance towards God, and faith towards our Lord Jesus Christ (Acts 10:21), and sincere obedience to his gospel (Rom. 2:7).

I am willing to go out of my flesh, and look to Jesus for righteousness and strength, and trust my salvation wholly on this foundation (Phil. 3:3-10). I am content to deal upon trust, and venture all in the hope of what is to come, and to tarry till the next world for my preferment (2 Cor. 5:7; 4:18). I am willing to wait till the coming of our Lord Jesus Christ, and have laid up my happiness on the other side the grave (1 Thess. 1:9, 10; Titus 2:13; Heb. 10:34; 11:35).

And though my sins be many, yet I should go against my own knowledge, if I should say they were not my constant trouble and burden (Rom. 7:24; Gal. 5:17), and the enemies against which I daily watch, and with whom my soul has no peace (Psa. 39:1; 17:3). My own heart knows that I hate them, and desire and endeavour their utter destruction, and do resolve against them all, and am willing to use all God's means (that I know of) to mortify them (Psa. 119:101, 104). It is too true that I often fall and fail; yet my conscience bears me witness that I confess and bewail it, and do not ordinarily and deliberately allow myself in any sin whatsoever against my knowledge (Rom. 7:15, 16, *etc.*; 1 Cor. 9:26, 27; 1 John 1:9; Rom. 6:16). And though my obedience be miserably lame, yet, O Lord, you know, that I have respect towards all your commandments (Psa. 119:6), and strive to come up to what you require (Psa. 119:5, 30, 173; 2 Cor. 5:9; Psa. 19:13; 119:133). The Holy Spirit is witness, and my conscience also, that I first seek the kingdom of God and its righteousness (Matt. 6:33), and that it is my chief care to please God, and keep from sin (Psa. 19:13; 119:133). Speak, O my soul, is not holiness your design? Do you not thirst for it, and follow after it? Do you not in your settled choice prefer the holy ways of God before all the pleasures and delights of sin? You know it is thus, and therefore no more disputing; you have sincerely taken hold of God's covenant, and without controversy it must be yours.

O my God, I see you have been at work with my soul. I find the prints, I see the footsteps. Surely this is the finger of God. I am your servant, O Lord, truly I am your servant (Psa. 116:16), and my soul has said to the Lord, You are my Lord (Psa. 16:2). It must be so. Would you ever set your mark upon another's goods? Or shall God disown his own workmanship? My name is written in heaven. You have written your name upon my heart, and therefore I cannot question but you have my name on your heart. I have chosen you, O Lord, as my happiness and inheritance, and therefore I am sure you have chosen me; for I could not have loved you, except you had loved me first (1 John 4:19; Hab. 2:3). O my Lord, discern, I pray you, whose are these, the signet, the bracelets, and the staff. I know you will acknowledge them.

Faith makes its claim to all the benefits of the covenant, and stirs up the soul to joy and thankfulness.

And now blessed be God, and the Father of our Lord Jesus Christ, who, of his abundant mercy, has begotten me into a living hope.

And you, my soul, believe and wait, look through the window, and cry through the lattice, and rejoice in the hope of the glory of God. The vision is for an appointed time, wait for it. It will come in the end, and will not tarry (Hab. 2:3). Behold, the husbandman waits for the precious fruits of the earth (James 5:7). You also be patient. He has long patience, and will you not have a little patience? He, for the fruits of the earth; but you, for the joys of heaven. He, upon mere probabilities; but you, upon infallible certainties. He, for a crop of corn, but you for a crown of glory. Were he but sure that every corn would bear a crown, how plentifully would he sow, how joyfully would he wait! Why, such is your harvest. As sure as the summer's delights follow the winter's severities; as sure as the wished-for harvest follows the toilsome and costly seed time, so sure shall your Lord return, and bring your reward with him (Rev. 22:12). Therefore, my soul, love and long for the approaching jubilee, and wait all the days of my appointed time, until my change shall come.

O blessed state that my Lord has translated me into! O happy change that he has made! I was a stranger, and he took me in and made me an heir; and preferred me from the dunghill to the throne, and from a hewer of wood and drawer of water, to attend his court, and know his counsels, and do his pleasure. Happy am I that ever I was born to partake of this endless dignity.

O my Lord, it is no little thing you have given me in hand. I am already come to Mount Zion, and the city of the living God, the heavenly Jerusalem, and to an innumerable company of angels, to the general assembly and church of the firstborn, and to God the Judge of all, and to the spirits of just men made perfect, and to Jesus the Mediator of the new covenant, and to the blood of sprinkling (Heb. 12:22-24). My heart revives as Jacob's, when I behold the tokens which you have sent me, the spirit of adoption (Gal. 4:6), the pardon of my sins (Luke 5:20), my patent for heaven (Luke 12:32), the chain of your graces (Song of Sol. 1:10), the Son of your bosom, the new covenant in his blood (1 Cor. 11:25), and the letters of his love (John 3:16). My Lord has said, that he will love me, and manifest himself to me; and that the Father will love me, and both will come to me, and make their abode in me (John 14:21, 23). But is it true indeed? Will the Lord dwell on earth? Or if he will, shall so foul a stable, so unclean a place as my heart has been, shall this be the place that the Lord of life will take up his lodging and keep his court in? Will he indeed come with all his train of graces, and live and walk in me? How can these things be? But he has said it, and I do, and I will believe it.

Yet all this is but the deposit which guarantees what is to come. O how great is your goodness, laid up for those who fear you! (Psa. 31:19). Yet a little, and my warfare shall be accomplished, and the heavens must receive me, till the time of the restitution of all things. It is but for a short term that I shall dwell in this flesh, in an earthen tabernacle (2 Pet. 1:14). My Lord has shown me, that where he is, there shall his servant be (John 12:26). Now the living is tied to the dead; and my soul is a stage of strife and a field of war. But it is but a little moment, and that which is perfect shall come (1 Cor. 13:10). Perfect holiness and perfect peace; eternal serenity and a serene eternity.

O my sins, I am going where you cannot come; where no unclean thing shall enter, nor any thing that defiles (Rev. 21:27). I think I see all my afflictions and temptations, all my infirmities and corruptions falling off me, as Elijah's cloak at his translation.

O my soul, do you not see the chariots of fire, and the horses of fire, come to take you up? Though you be as poor as Lazarus (Luke 16:22), yet God will not disdain to send a party of angels to conduct you home. How can you doubt of a ready reception, who has such a Friend in court, who will lead you with boldness into his Father's presence? If there was joy in Pharaoh's court, when it was said, Joseph's brethren are come (Gen. 45:16), surely it will be welcome news in heaven, when it is told, Jesus's brethren are come.

My soul, fear not to enter, though the Lord be clothed with terror and majesty: for your Redeemer will procure you favour, and plead your right. I am sure of a welcome, for the Father himself loves me (John 16:27). I have tasted and tried his love; and when I had played the wicked prodigal (Luke 15), yet he despised not my rags, but fell on my neck and kissed me, and heaven itself rejoiced over me. Much more will he receive me gladly, and let out his love upon me, when presented to him by his Son, in his perfect likeness, as a fit object for his everlasting delight. Fear not, O my soul, as if you were going to a strange place. Why, heaven is your country and your home: will you doubt your right to enter, or fear you will not receive a welcome, when it is your own home? Why, my soul, you were born from above, and here is your kindred and your Father's house, and therefore you shall surely be admitted. And then shall I see the glorious preparations of eternal love, and the blissful mansions of the heavenly inhabitants.

Doubtless it will be thus. These are not sick men's dreams, or children's hopes. The living God cannot deceive me: and may I not certainly promise myself what the Lord has promised me? I will sooner think that all my senses are deluded, and what I see and feel and taste is but a fancy, than think that the living God will deceive me, or that his unchangeable covenant will fail. Now I am a son of God, and it does not yet appear what I shall be: but this I know, I shall be like him, and see him as he is (1 John 3:2).

I know it shall be thus. Why, what security should I ask of God? He has given me all the assurance in the word. And though the word of God is enough, yet he, willing to show more abundantly to the heirs of promise the immutability of his counsel, confirmed it by an oath: that by two immutable things, in which it was impossible for God to lie, I might have strong consolation (Heb. 6:17, 18). O unreasonable unbelief! What! shall not the oath of God put an end to your strife?

O my God, I am satisfied: it is enough. Now I may be bold without presumption, and boast without pride. And will no more call my duty arrogance, nor my faith a fancy.

O my soul! there is but a short life between you and glory, where holy angels, and glorified saints, shall be my associates, and love and praise my only employment. I think I hear already how the morning stars sing together, and all the sons of God shout for joy (Job 38:7). O that I could come in for one! But it was said to me, that I should rest yet for a little season, but I shall stand in my lot at the end of the days (Dan. 12:13).

It is well, Lord, your word is enough; your bond is as good as ready payment. The Holy Spirit tells me, that life and glory wait patiently for me; that the very day I am loosed from the body, that same day I shall be landed in paradise. Amen (Luke 23:43). It is as I would have it.

But this is not all. When my body has slept a short nap in the dust, Christ will call to it, Come up hither. Ah, true yoke-fellow, it will be a hard parting, but a welcome meeting. I could not leave you but to live with Christ (Col. 3:4). But he will raise you a glorious temple; and when he shall appear, will bring me with himself in glory; and then I shall re-enter you as a royal mansion, in which I shall abide with the Lord for ever. For as we have served our Redeemer together, so we must be glorified together with him. And when the Lord has married us together again, then will he marry us both unto himself. For I know that my Redeemer lives, and that he shall stand at the last day over the earth. And though after my skin, worms destroy this body, yet in my flesh I shall see God; whom I shall see for myself, and my eyes shall behold, and not another, though my heart is consumed within me. My Lord has already told me how it shall be. He has set down the time, and shown me the robes of immortality and the crown of life that I must put on; and the throne of glory, and the seat of judgment that I must sit on. He has told me the manner in which I shall be presented to him, and espoused by him. He has told me where he will set me, and what he will say to me, and how he will acknowledge my mean services, and remember what I have forgotten (Matt. 25:35, 37), how he will praise the works that I have been ashamed of, and reward me openly for what I have buried in secrecy (Matt. 6:4), and not forget the poorest alms that I have given for his name. Then will he confess me before his Father, and before the angels of God. Thus says the true and faithful witness, and we know that his testimony is true.

Ah, my soul, see that you do not make God a liar (1 John 5:10).

O my God, I have believed your report, and look for all these things, according to your promise. I know you intend me to remain in this lower region for just a very little while. This world is but the house of my pilgrimage, and my soul now is but like a bird in the shell; but when the shell is cracked, then shall she take wings like a dove, and soar aloft to you, and fly away, and be at rest.

Yet I do not doubt your care for my despicable dust (John 6:39). I know that nothing will be lost; I know not where they will lay me: but your wakeful eye observes, and will not have to seek at what door to knock, nor at what grave to call, for me. I believe, and am sure that I shall come a glorious piece out of your hands, fair as the moon, clear as the sun, crowned with honour and glory. And when my absolution is read, and sentence past upon the world, then must I be taken up to dwell with you.

Let not my Lord be angry, that your dust and ashes speaks thus to you. You Lord have raised my expectations, and have made me look for all these great things from you. In vain have you written all these things to me, if I should not believe them; and a distrustful diffidence would put a high dishonour upon your truth.

O Lord, I repent; I repent of my jealousies, and my doubtful thoughts about you. I know you love a humble confidence, and delight in nothing more than to see your children trust you. I know the building of my hopes lies not a hair's breadth over the foundation of your promises, yes, it is sure, my expectations are infinitely short of what I shall find.

O my God, my heart trusts safely in you, and I here set to my seal that you are true (John 3:33). Christ is the cornerstone on which I build (Eph. 2:20), and therefore my building will challenge the winds and floods.

And now, O Lord, what am I waiting for? My hope is in you (Psa. 39:7). O my blessedness, let me enjoy you. O my life, let me possess you. O desire of my eyes, let me see your face and hear your voice; for your voice is sweet, and your countenance is beautiful. I ask but what you have promised: for you have told me that I shall see God, and you will speak to me mouth to mouth (Matt. 5:8), even apparently, and not in dark speeches, and the similitude of God shall I behold.

So shall my knowledge be perfected (1 Cor. 13:9, 10), and I shall see the inaccessible light, and my tender eye shall not water, nor my sight dazzle; but I shall with open face look steadfastly on the sun of righteousness, and behold his glory. Then shall faith be turned into fruition, and hope into possession, and love shall arise like the full moon in her brightness, and never wax nor wane more.

O God of my hopes, I look for a new body, and a new soul; for new heavens, and for a new earth, according to your promise; when my whole soul shall be wholly taken up with you, and all my affections strained to the highest pitch, and all the wheels of my raised powers set in most vigorous and perpetual motion towards you, still letting in, and still laying out; and thus shall there be an everlasting communication of joy and glory from you, and of love and praise from me.

O my soul, you are rich indeed, and increased in goods. You have no reason to envy the glory or grandeur of the mightiest on earth: for their glory shall not descend after them; like sheep shall they be laid in their graves, and death shall feed upon them, and there is an eternal end of all their pomp and excellency. But my kingdom is an everlasting kingdom. My robes shall never wear, my crown shall never totter, my throne shall never be vacant, my bread shall never decay, my garland shall never wither, my house shall never moulder, my wine shall never sour, but everlasting joy shall be upon my head, and sorrow and sighing shall fly away.

O my God, how happy have you made me! It is better than I could have wished. You have done all things well. You have settled them for ever. The whole earth cannot show any such inheritance or tenure. The world can confer her possessions but only for a few years, nor can she make a good title for that neither. But my inheritance is for ever, and none can put me out of possession. The thing is established in heaven, and in the volume of the book it is written of me. My evidence cannot be lost; it is recorded in the court above, and enrolled in the sacred leaves of the word, and entered upon the book of my conscience, and in this I do and will rejoice.

Now, my soul, wipe your eyes, and go away with Hannah, and be sad no more. What though my house be not so with God, so happy, so prosperous as I could wish? What though they be increased that trouble me, and my temptations and afflictions are like the rolling billows, riding on one another's backs for haste? Yet shall my soul be as a rock unmoved, and shall sit down satisfied in the security and amplitude of my portion. For God has made with me an everlasting covenant, ordered in all things, and sure; and in this is all my salvation, and all my desire.

And now, what remains, O Lord, but that I should spend the remainder of my days in loving, praising, and admiring you? But with what shall I come before the Lord, or bow myself to the most high God? What shall I give you, to express my thankfulness, though not to requite your bounty? Alas, my poor little soul! Alas you are so little! How narrow are your capacities! How disproportionate are your powers! Alas that my voice can reach to no higher a note! But shall I do nothing because I cannot do all?

Lord, I resign to you. With the poor widow, I cast my two mites, my soul and body, into your treasury. All my powers shall love and serve you. All my members shall be weapons of righteousness for you. Here is my good will. Behold, my substance is your stock, mine interest is for your service. I lay all at your feet: there, you have them, they are yours. My children I enter as your servants. My possessions I resign as your right. I will call nothing mine but you. All mine are yours. I can say, My Lord and my God, and that is enough; I thankfully quit my claim to everything else. I will no more say, My house is mine, or my estate mine; I myself am not my own. Yet it is infinitely better for me to be yours, than if I were my own. This is my happiness, that I can say, My own God, my own Father. And oh what a blessed exchange have you made with me! to give me yourself, who are an infinite sum, for myself, who am but an insignificant cipher.

And now, Lord, accept and own my claim. I am not worthy of anything of yours, much less of you. But since I have a deed to show, I bring your word in my hand, and am bold to take possession. Do you not know this hand? Will you not own this name? Will you not confirm your own grant? It were infidelity to doubt it. I will not disparage the faithfulness of my Lord, nor be afraid to aver, and stand to what he has said and sworn. Have you said you are my God, and shall I fear you are my enemy? Have you told me you are my Father, and shall I stand aloof, as if I were a stranger? I will believe. Lord, silence my fears; and as you have given me the claim and title of a child, so give me the confidence of a child. Let my heart be daily kept alive by your promises, and with this staff let me pass over Jordan. May these be my undivided companions and comforters. When I go, let them lead me; when I sleep, let them keep me; when I awake, let them talk with me. And keep these things for ever upon the imaginations of the thoughts of the hearts of your people, and prepare their hearts for you. And let the heart of your servant be the ark of your testament, in which the sacred records of what has passed between you and my soul may for ever be preserved. Amen. Thus far my friend. So be it.

THE END.